Law of Attraction and Weight Loss

Practical Steps to Change Your Mindset, Lose Weight and Finally Manifest Your Dream Body

2nd EDITION

Nathan Powers

© **Copyright 2014 by Nathan Powers - All rights reserved.**

In no way is it legal to reproduce, duplicate, or transmit any part of this document in either electronic means or in printed format. Recording of this publication is strictly prohibited and any storage of this document is not allowed unless with written permission from the publisher. All rights reserved.

The information provided herein is stated to be truthful and consistent, in that any liability, in terms of inattention or otherwise, by any usage or abuse of any policies, processes, or directions contained within is the solitary and utter responsibility of the recipient reader. Under no circumstances will any legal responsibility or blame be held against the publisher for any reparation, damages, or monetary loss due to the information herein, either directly or indirectly.

Respective authors own all copyrights not held by the publisher.

Legal Notice:

This book is copyright protected. This is only for personal use. You cannot amend, distribute, sell, use, quote or paraphrase any part or the content within this book without the consent of the author or copyright owner. Legal action will be pursued if this is breached.

Disclaimer Notice:

Nathan Powers

Please note the information contained within this document is for educational and entertainment purposes only. Every attempt has been made to provide accurate, up to date and reliable complete information. No warranties of any kind are expressed or implied. Readers acknowledge that the author is not engaging in the rendering of legal, financial, medical or professional advice.

By reading this document, the reader agrees that under no circumstances are we responsible for any losses, direct or indirect, which are incurred as a result of the use of information contained within this document, including, but not limited to, — errors, omissions, or inaccuracies.

Table of Contents

ABOUT THE AUTHOR 7

INTRODUCTION 11

CHAPTER 1 - THE LAW OF ATTRACTION – WHAT IS IT? 15

CHAPTER 2 - THE LAW OF ATTRACTION AND PHYSICS 21

CHAPTER 3 - LAW OF ATTRACTION AND LOSING WEIGHT 27

CHAPTER 4 – MAKING A VISION BOARD 33

CHAPTER 5 – HOW LOSING WEIGHT WITH THE LAW OF ATTRACTION AFFECTS WHAT YOU EAT 37

CHAPTER 6 - HOW TO MAKE USE OF LAW OF ATTRACTION PRINCIPLES TO LOSE WEIGHT 41

CHAPTER 7 - HOW VIBRATIONS INFUSIONS CAN HELP YOU LOSE WEIGHT 49

CHAPTER 8 - APPLYING THE LAW OF APPARENCY IN WEIGHT LOSS 57

HOW IT WORKS 61

CHAPTER 9 – KEEPING THE WEIGHT OFF 65

CHAPTER 10 – WHERE THOUGHTS COME FROM AND WHAT THEY DO 77

CHAPTER 11 – FOOD, DRINK AND EXERCISE 87

CONCLUSION 91

CHECK OUT MY OTHER BOOKS 93

About The Author

I got into Law of Attraction in 2006 (I thought) quite by accident, though now I know better. That's the problem. You never know it's hitting you until it does.

Growing up, I never imagined that I would have the life I have now. I was raised in a beaten down neighborhood in the midwest with more problems then I knew how to handle. My mother left my father after his abuse and womanizing became too much. The broken marriage itself had the effect of leaving me worried that I would never have a solid relationship of my own and lost because I rejected my father's idea of manhood.

In between the drinking that I had turned to in order to dull my emotions, I would spend hours reading. It was there in the library that I ran into my first life-changing book, *"Think and Grow Rich"* by Napoleon Hill. It was to become a turning point in my life, which is why I want to share my experience with others.

I started tackling my own limiting thoughts, listening to and creating powerful affirmations for myself about wealth, abundance, relationships and success. I radically changed my daily habits and learned the mind disciplines that I needed in order to thrive. After taking countless classes, seminars, reading books and traveling to conferences, I've studied as much as I could on the powerful Law of Attraction with the hopes of sharing it with others.

While I'm not (yet) a millionaire, I now live a life that I never dreamed I could have. I have the business and productivity I've always wanted, have transformed my body and found the partner of my dreams. I now know that I can have anything I want by manifesting the thought and feeling of it so clearly, that I can sit in the peace of that fulfillment and make it so in the tangible universe. It's it own form of "work" and it takes practice, but I am dedicated to sharing all I know with you so that you may also have the life you truly want.

I've studied program after program and am also committed to

sharing with you tips, strategies and products that I believe will serve you powerfully on your journey towards becoming a master of manifestation. I wish some of these had been around earlier!

You can have the life of your dreams, if you're willing to clear the clutter and garbage that's been taking up space in your mind and replace it with powerful affirmations, thoughts and habits that will have you transforming your brain and life forever!

Enjoy,

Nathan Powers

Nathan Powers

Introduction

I want to thank you and congratulate you for buying the book, ***"Law of Attraction and Weight Loss: Practical Steps to Change Your Mindset, Lose Weight and Finally Manifest your Dream Body, 2nd Edition"***.

This book contains proven steps and strategies on how to lose weight and have the body you've always dreamed of by using the Law of Attraction to help you. The Law of Attraction isn't something new. It's always been there and is explained in detail within the pages of this book because the author is conversant with all of the powers that can be gleaned from it.

Do you know that you can do anything that you set your mind to do? Do you know that by setting your mind and thoughts to do something, you are simply using the law of attraction? When you set your mind to do something, you simply align your thoughts to what you want to achieve. Since the law of attraction states that like begets like, you will manifest what you set your mind to do. This book would be very helpful to you as it explains how you can lose weight with the law of attraction. You will also learn how to effectively use several law of attraction principles to achieve your dream body.

We all want to look the best that we can. However, it's not always possible because we put too many hurdles in the way of our own success. This book shows you how to use your inner energies to devote them to believing in yourself and thus empowering the Law of Attraction to give you the body you always wanted. Once you learn how to do this, you will wonder why you never discovered its simplicity before. The point is that life throws too many hurdles into our pathway right from the moments of childhood. You may not know it, but your thoughts may be exactly what are getting in the way of really making the most of who you are. Learn through reading this book how you can change all that.

Thanks again for buying this book, I hope you enjoy it and I also hope that you gain positive benefits from your choice of book. This book is written with you in mind and if you have been struggling to get yourself into shape, you have come to the right place. You never know what help is out there unless you are prepared to take the road to discovery. This book promises you results that you will be happy with.

Nathan Powers

Chapter 1 - The Law of Attraction – What Is It?

Have you heard of the law of attraction before? Are you wondering what it is? Do you have any idea of the principles surrounding this law? Have you read books related with the theory? Do you believe in this concept? Read on to get all your questions answered.

The law of attraction is a concept that involves the idea that the events that happen around us are a direct manifestation of the thoughts that circulate in our minds. The law of attraction works on the principle that everything including thoughts and people are actually made of energy particles. This is why they are interrelated on both levels.

The universe has no way to understand and assess as to whether your activities and events are in accordance with what you want. Depending upon the kind of thoughts and energy vibration, which you have, the events and activities that occur will be the same as the universe simply matches the energy molecules. The vibration, which your thought energy has, is always the same as those of the actual events that occur. The principle of vibration infusion comes into play here since it explains why interacting with vibrations that are different from you will infuse the new vibrations in your life. This simply means if you are poor and start vibrating positive energy towards being rich, you will ultimately manifest experiences to match with the infused vibrations manifesting richness. While this may seem intriguing, you can only make the most out of law of attraction principles if you have a strong belief in them.

Your Belief in the Principle Must be Unwavering

Even if you are new to the law of attraction, you first need to have an unwavering belief in it. If you have a shaky belief, your thoughts will not have positive vibration and energy and so things won't work the way you have envisioned them to.

The entire success of application of law of energy relies on the fact that everything ranging from your thoughts to the actions and even the events are nothing but forms of energy. This is why the thoughts that you think are finally mapped into the energy molecules of the physical events that actually occur. The mapping is done per se which infers that the type of thoughts that circulate in your mind will be directly mapped to the outer events that will occur in your real space.

The thoughts that circulate your mind have a certain sense of energy and the events that occur are a direct manifestation of the energy molecules. They are mapped directly from one stratum to the others.

However, if your belief in these principles is not up to the mark, it will lead to confusion and your energy vibration will not be in tandem with what you desire. As per the laws of attraction, you should think of things you want to achieve. When you are surrounding yourself with the right type of thoughts, you are likely to experience the same things and thus you will get the best output that you have been waiting for.

The Law of Attraction relates to every area of your life and that's not just weight loss. It applies to money, to love life and to everything that you do within your life. The energy of the Law of Attraction is always there for you to cling to, but you need to be on the same energy level as it for you to gain all the benefits available to you. One word of caution is that if you don't believe in yourself or you have doubts, the Law of Attraction won't work. You have to at some stage in your life take a leap of faith and if you really want your world to improve, now is the best time to make that decision. Let negative thoughts out of your mind, even if people have been teasing you for years about your weight. It's not your responsibility to live up to other people's expectations and the sooner you realize that the better. When you try to do that, you load yourself up with the potential of disappointment.

However, when you see how the Law of Attraction works for you, you can lose weight for yourself and for yourself alone. Your body is your responsibility and by believing in it and in your own ability to take on life at full throttle and in a totally positive way, you can get over all the stigma attached to weight and watch the pounds drop off. One of the reasons that so many people fail to grasp the concept of the Law of Attraction is because they harbor negative thoughts and have thus never experienced it. To them, because it doesn't work, it doesn't exist. However, I've got news for you. The Universe lends its energy to anyone who is open minded enough to grasp it and that includes you. Banish negative thoughts from your mind. Forget about all your dieting failures and start to think of the Law of Attraction as your friend because it really is and it really can help you to lose weight.

If you are not on the same frequency as the Law of Attraction, it will never work, but it's as easy as child's play. What you need to do is drop all negative activity. That means finding your true center and your place of happiness and not let anyone take away that positivity. With the Law of Attraction, like always attracts like. Your positive attitude will draw the Law of Attraction into your life and help you in your plight to lose weight, just as it can help you in all other areas of your life.

Nathan Powers

Chapter 2 - The Law of Attraction and Physics

Some people argue that there is no scientific basis to the principles of law of attraction; however, it is not so. The basis of the law of attraction is hidden in the dynamics of energy. When we are talking of energy particles and their vibration, we can derive knowledge from laws of physics.

The origin of both physics and mathematics lies in the theory that the universe is infinite and the law of attraction is in effect at all times. At the deeper core level, the universe is nothing but a ball of energy. All the different laws of physics fall back on this concept that energy gives you the base upon which we carry out the rest of our assumptions. The law of attraction runs on the same principles too and thus all the laws of physics, big or small are in a way related to the law of attraction. So, if you are one of those who need logic to believe that law of attraction has a scientific proof, you need to know that physics and mathematics offer you the right proof for this law.

When you are breaking down substances to get to the base of matter, you will find that everything ranging from the tiniest molecule to even the largest animal is ultimately composed of energy particles. As per this principle, the events that happen to you are a direct manifestation of the thoughts, which are present in your mind. The logic behind the same is the principle of energy molecules. The energy molecules of your ongoing thoughts should be in tandem with the expected molecules and the right energy band that you desire.

The most important law of physics which is "energy is neither created nor destroyed" also forms the basis of the law of attraction, as the energy molecules are merely mapped, so your thoughts will be directly mapped to the output which you will get. The amount of energy that the universe possesses is infinite. Therefore, you should ideally work upon the different dynamics that will help you in making the most out of your energy vibrations.

You have to tune your thoughts to start vibrating within the same vibrational frequency of whatever you want manifested in your life; in this case, if you want to lose weight, being in a vibrational zone that makes you vibrate a life when you are already fit can make you attract fitness in your life. Although it can be hard to maneuver the energy vibrations that you have, the law of attraction has several tips and exercises that will actually allow you to control your energy zones and vibrations. If you believe in logic, physics and mathematics, it is the energy principle that is going to guide you into making the most out of the law of attraction principles.

So how does this work for weight loss?

It works in exactly the same way as it does for gaining wealth or for being successful. You need positively charged energy to get in touch with the Law of Attraction and must always remember the keywords. Like attracts like. Thus, if you want to be slim, you have to think slim. You have to actually feel that you are losing weight and stick to what you believe no matter what feedback you get from others.

Keeping away from people who make you feel fat is the first way to lift your energies, but there are much more than that. You can make yourself a vision board and this is very valuable for the Law of Attraction. On this board, you place things like pictures of the ideal weight that you want to be and every time you look at the board, you concentrate all your energy into actually being that person that you see in the image.

People use vision boards for all kinds of visions and that includes wanting money, material possession, happiness or anything within their lives that can be provided by linking up energy with the Law of Attraction. If you think slim, you will become slim. If you think fat – you will remain fat. If you think anything negative – you will feel negative.

The idea of the vision board is to remind you of who you are – not who you wish to become. It's whom you feel you are inside. For example, I see myself as reasonably tall and don't have a potbelly. I have a nice tight behind and I can stand straight and look great when I dress up. It isn't a case of convincing yourself or playing role-play. It's a case of believing totally in your ability to be this person that you have in photographic format on your vision board.

Things you cannot change

You have to learn to accept the things that you cannot change because if you feel that these let you down, you can't think positively and that works against you. You need to be positive at all times. Look into the mirror at your body. You cannot change your hair type but you can change the style if you wish you. You can't change the length of your legs so there's not much point in fretting about them. In fact, all of the things that you were born with and that cannot change don't even bear thinking about because it is all wasted energy. In other words, if you want to slim down, you first need to eliminate all of the things that you have so far seen as negative. You can't change them. Forget about having a complex about them because it changes nothing. All it does is make you feel bad about something that is essentially you and that will never change short of having surgery. Look around you and wake up. People are born with flaws and they don't all mope about them. Accept those things that you can't change because they are just part of who you are.

You also need to accept why you want to lose weight and keep your aims in mind so that you are positive during the whole process. The problem is that the Law of Attraction won't work all on its own. You have to meet it half way. When you find that balance that puts you in control of your life, it's amazing. I must say that it took a while to understand the physics of it. I was never that good at sciences at school but someone put it into diagram format for me and it was extremely helpful and I could see how logical it was that if you are not on the same energy wave as the Universe, you can't really gain anything at all. We are all one mass of energy and sometimes negative energy is allowed to take precedence over positive energy. That's when things go wrong.

If you have ever dieted in the past and have the experience of yoyo dieting or failure, then you will have experienced the negative energy that goes with it. After all, going without all your favorite foods, you expect to get results and when, in a couple of weeks' time you put all that weight back on again, it hardly seems fair.

Things you can change

You can change your attitude. That's going to be one of the most important changes that you make. In a future chapter, we will discuss how this helps you and what it does to help the Law of Attraction to work its magic. Once you learn how easy it is, you will wonder why you never did it before. It's not about feeling deprived. You need to work toward something positive and see all the positive sides of being fit and healthy. That's the bit you need to tune into because it's all positive stuff and will keep you in its grasp while you change the shape of your body for the better.

Chapter 3 - Law of Attraction and Losing Weight

As per the law of attraction, you merely need to think the things that you crave if you want them to manifest in your life. So, if you are looking to shed the extra pounds, all you really need to do is believe that you are already thin and you have a great body that people admire. When you keep murmuring these thoughts to yourself and put away the depressing thoughts of not weighing what you want, you will actually be able to get the body you have been craving for. Isn't this better than staying hungry all day, opting for crash dieting or spending three hours at the gym? What is the harm in trying it out?

Gone are the days when you needed to give up your favorite foods just to lose a few pounds. Knowing how to vibrate the right kind of energy through changing your thoughts will help you get rid of the extra pounds that you have accumulated. Therefore, you can get the slim shape, which you have been craving for. You can eat your favorite food, skip exercises on days you have no stamina to run and simply carve your thoughts in the right direction.

Losing weight is as much a mental thing as a physical one. If you have the confidence of cutting down your extra flab, nothing can stop you from doing it. We'll take a look at some practical strategies to use if you want to enter into the vibrational zone of being fit, which will ultimately make it easy for you to lose weight.

Relationship between your mindset and losing weight

The mindset you have will determine whether you will lose weight or not. The thoughts you have about your weight determine the nature of vibrations you will have and the kind of manifestations that will happen in your life. Simply put, if you want to attract your desires, you have to maintain a mindset that matches your desires. This means that if you want to lose weight, you need to have a mindset of being fit and being able to do all those things that you may not have been able to do probably because you are overweight.

If you want to shed off those pounds, you need to adopt an appropriate mindset. You cannot have a mindset of defeat, despair and desperation, as this is likely to make you stressed and even lead to weight gain especially if you are the kind of person who is an emotional eater. Being happy and positive is the only way that you are going to attract being fit and happy. Just try it and you will not look back. In any case, what does being depressed and sad add to you? I bet more misery and heartache. Try to adopt a positive mindset even for just a week; the results will be amazing.

What kind of changes do you need to make?

When you decide for good that you want a better figure, you change mindset. Instead of being quite happy to put away the calories, you tend to use a vision board for encouragement and to remind you of what the aim is. This can be something that you don't need to share with anyone else. It's a private thing. Don't add to your unhappiness by trying to measure up to other people's expectations because when you do that in conjunction with weight loss, you tend to set yourself up for failure.

You have to be in this because you want to be in it. Thus, you know the common sense ruling about what's acceptable and what's not acceptable, but the Law of Attraction means that if you already believe yourself to be slim and pretty, the chances are that you will be attracted to foods that actively encourage that. Try your hand at experimentation, but remember that nothing about losing weight in this scenario must be negative. If you find it too hard to resist a temptation, bend to it a little, but not as much as you usually do. A slim and fit lady or man wouldn't eat a whole donut. Therefore, take a bite and keep the rest for another time. That way, you don't have to deprive yourself of anything. You are merely thinking like a thin person and keeping very positive while you do this.

The law of attraction works when you keep a positive mindset. Put the scales away. It's not about you measuring up or being disappointed when you have a bad day. It's about being very happy to be who you are and knowing in your heart of hearts that you can slim down to the weight that you want to be. If you keep showing yourself the positive results of your effort by seeing pictures of what you really are inside, rather than what people see from the outside, you really can keep achieving. Think slim. You are slim inside. Now all you need to do is get the outside to catch up. Don't make promises to anyone. This isn't about anyone else at all. It is between you and the picture that you have pinned to your vision board. The point is that you are giving yourself a direction and you are continually positive about it because you know that's really who you are on the inside.

In the next chapter, we are going to go through the use of a vision board because this is very important to the whole process. The vision board is your contact with the Universe. It's your starting point for gathering the right kind of energy that you need for the Law of Attraction to work. Without this energy, you won't succeed, so try not to skip this stage. It's vital and will ensure that you succeed in your efforts.

Nathan Powers

Chapter 4 – Making A Vision Board

A vision board is very useful when you want to get in touch with your inner feelings because what you need to do is construct it and place it in a place where you can contemplate it. In the case of losing weight, the obvious place to put it would be on the fridge or the dining table or breakfast bar – wherever you come into contact with food. The positive thing about this is that it reinforces that feeling that you are slim. Stop looking at your body. You really have to imagine yourself slim to think slim. Remember, like attracts like.

To construct the board, you can buy a sheet of polypropylene from a local store, but try to make sure that you can put push pins into it and that it's thick enough so that the pins do not come out the other side. Now, open some magazines and be as realistic as you can about the figure that you want. You need to see this at

33

least three times a day and contemplate on it, so fill the board with lots of nice pictures of how you see your inner self. Remember, you have to believe in yourself and these pictures show you how you see yourself if you want to become slim again. Other things that you can stick on the board to help you are things like delicious fruit, recipes which are delicious but not particularly high in calories.

Get rid of your scales. The idea is not to be disappointed every time you weigh yourself. You can lose weight but if you keep reinforcing negative disappointments into your energy stream, you are unlikely to last and certainly less able to get in touch with enough high energy to use the Law of Attraction. You have to understand that the Law of Attraction does not understand and is repelled by negativity of any sort at all.

Although you are free to eat what you want to, when you look at your vision board and see how you look, you might find that you automatically make different choices. After all, you are not the fatty you once were and slim people don't pile up their plates with foods that make them feel sluggish and lacking in energy. Your new slim self may also be pleased to exercise in a gym or even at home. Dancing to a Zumba video is great fun. Imagine yourself as the lithe person that you see yourself as on your vision board and you will soon pump out energy that you didn't know you had and feel really good as well.

The vision board is your reminder of who you now are. You don't have to discuss it with anyone. You don't have to justify it. It's your private place to go and contemplate and as you look at each of the pictures, remind yourself of what you are doing and let the positive energy flow. Don't even go there if you feel negative because negativity doesn't work and will lead to more negativity. You have to totally believe in you when you sit down and look at the pictures on the board. Say things while you point to pictures, such as:

- I have a great waistline
- I have great hips
- My chest is looking slim
- My breasts are firm and lovely
- My legs are shapely
- I love fruit and vegetables

- I thrive on positivity

You have to repeat these mantras as much as you can and see yourself as this slim person because slim people don't tend to slouch when they sit and you will automatically sit better. Slim people don't stick their stomach out and you will find yourself automatically pulling your tummy in. You will be less lazy and find yourself with more energy than you usually have based on the fact that you are slim and believe it. You are not lying, as each of the pictures on the vision board was based upon how you see yourself inside. Now, all you need to do is adjust the outside so that you look super cool and slim.

Remember that your vision board is there to remind you of who you are – not who you want to be. If you want to be something else, this usually involves jealousy and that's a really negative thing to feel right now. Be that person. Feel that self-love and thrive on it, because it's going to get you results and faster than you may imagine.

Chapter 5 – How Losing Weight with the Law of Attraction Affects What You Eat

We have told you in previous chapters that you can eat what you want to eat. The point is though that if you are a slim person, you need less food. You don't have that yearn to eat all the things that are high in calories. You may even find that you are happy to perform the odd fast because it really gets your muscle tone looking nice and makes you appreciate everything that you do eat. You have to tell yourself when you sit down to eat that you are a slim person. Do slim people eat all of those French fries? Of course not. Thus, you need to do a little observation.

Go to a local restaurant and watch people. Look at slim people and watch what they eat. You are going to become one of them and it's important that you have the right energy levels to be able to let the Law of Attraction helps you to slim down the skin you're in. If they drink water, drink water. If they don't drink soda, find a great alternative because there are other drinks that are less harmful.

The reason this is so important is that it keeps your morale high while you are going through your metamorphosis. If you are slim and you eat all the bad foods that you ate before, you are likely to feel sluggish and negative because food weighs you down so much. I don't believe in diets at all. People who diet go through all that pain and at the end of the diet, when they go back to normal eating, tend to pile the pounds back on again. Thus, it is pretty pointless to tell you to give up foods that you like. However, ask yourself before you eat things "Does a slim person eat this?" and you might find you are much more conscious about what you eat without actually feeling deprived.

In the early days, it takes a bit of getting used to but you have to fit the role that you have taken on and if that means a little bit of change in your game plan, then it's all part of playing the role that you want to actually become. Reinforce positivity at all times that you can. Tell yourself how good you feel after a modified meal. Tell yourself how much energy you have and take yourself out as a treat for a walk in the park. You are a slim person and you enjoy walking especially if the weather is clement.

So what is the Law of Attraction doing for me?

The Law of Attraction is doing lots of things while you are being slim. It's changing your mindset. It's grabbing your positivity and adding to it. All of this energy and positivity will make you burn calories and will also make you more aware of your posture. You will feel strengthened by the fact that you are not going it alone. Whenever you feel a little negative, pick up the vision board and never lose sight of the vision. That's what keeps you going and what the Law of Attraction picks up on. People who believe in what they are doing gain from the law of attraction because like attracts like. You are positive, you are slim, and you are being the best person that you can be. In return the Law of Attraction helps you to become slim. Whether you feel it or not, whether you can talk to it or not – you are becoming slimmer with every day that passes because it responds to positive attitude and the way you are approaching your new slimness is totally positive.

There are no rules except those that you place in front of you. The Law of Attraction will work for you because you are thinking slim. People who think slim usually feel very proud of their bodies and they have every right to. Be proud of yours and let the energy flow because all this positive energy is burning away the person you used to be and making you a better person who will live longer and thrive and be able to pass that example to others.

If you don't lose weight straight away, it's because you are not concentrating hard enough on your vision board or saying the right things to yourself sufficiently. The point is that through life you are always reminded by others of your weaknesses. Now, you don't listen to others. You listen to your vision and that gives you a very different picture to the one painted by negative people. You see that waistline. You begin to celebrate being you and you will also begin to feel the health benefits and the thrill of actually feeling fitter and more capable of doing all the things that slim people do. That works for you because that's who you have now decided you are.

It will never be a case of deprivation. You choose what you eat, but slim people eat less. You choose how much you exercise, but slim people tend to have more energy and exercise more. You choose your future but what you don't see happening behind the scenes is that the Law of Attraction is keeping you going and persuading you behind the scenes by your energy levels that you really are a slim person and enjoy being one. There's no stigma. There's no shame. There's no negativity.

Chapter 6 - How to Make Use of Law of Attraction Principles to Lose Weight

We will look at some of the critical law of attraction principles that will catapult you into losing weight. Since the use of meditation is useful for you while you are using the Law of Attraction, I feel that learning to relax is probably a first step toward being able to meditate. Many people do not have the willpower to meditate so try breathing exercises and relaxation before you try your meditation.

To practice breathing correctly, close your eyes, breathe in through the nose, hold the breath for a moment and breathe out. You need to feel the air coming from the upper abdomen. Now try it again, but this time concentrate on the breathing and try not to think about anything else.

Relaxation

To practice relaxation, lie on a bed and have your pillow as low as possible so that you open your airways. You need to do this when you are alone and when you have no interruptions. Now concentrate on each part of the body from your toes right up to the top of your head, one at a time – tensing that part of the body and then relaxing it totally until you are in a state of relaxation. Don't get up quickly from this exercise. Simply get up in your own time as it takes your body a little while to adjust. When you have mastered this and done it several times, you will be ready to try meditation. There are several types of meditation and if you cannot do this sitting down, try it walking around because many people who are new to meditation find that this way works best for them.

Use meditation to focus on positive thoughts

Mediation holds the solution to a great deal of problems. Most people may not necessarily want to focus on negative thoughts but rather on positive ones. However, they do not have the power to refocus their attention from the negative thoughts to the positive thoughts. Meditation helps you to learn how to focus since you are usually required to go to a peaceful place, relax, breathe slowly and meditate for let's say twenty minutes. After any meditation session, you experience clarity in mind, which is key in enabling you to determine your specific desires relating to such issues of interest like weight loss. Additionally, meditation requires you not to concentrate on any thought as you meditate; it is the state of pure nothingness, which is bliss. As you become better at meditating, it becomes much easier to refocus your attention to positive thoughts rather than negative thoughts.

When you are meditating, you should not think of the repercussions of being fat.

Your main focus should be on feeling light, happy and beautiful. When you do so, you will align your thoughts in the same zone as the desired output. The more you have positive thoughts as compared to negative thoughts, the more the positive thoughts replace the negative thoughts. This is usually referred to as vibrational displacement. This means that you do not have to worry about the negative thoughts getting in the way of your progress. Although you should try to avoid negative thoughts, you can try having more positive thoughts that counter negative thoughts if it is too hard to get rid of all the negative thoughts.

For instance, if you have one negative thought of how it is impossible to lose weight, you can then decide to have several positive thoughts like how good you will look once you lose weight, how healthy you will be as well as how important it is to have your ideal weight. The more positive thoughts you have, the more the negative thoughts will be displaced and over time, you will have more positive thoughts as compared to negative thoughts. Remember at times like this to take your vision board with you so that you can look at it before your meditation begins and after it has finished. This will help you to regain that confidence that you have in the new slim you. This is very important and helps you to meditate in a more efficient manner and that's really useful to channeling your energy so that it falls into the energy of the universe around you.

The Universe is a Ball of Infinite Energy

You have the potential to talk to the universe. You can control the energy molecules. When sending out the signals to the universe, you will explain what you need from it. The energy vibrations that you are sending to the universe are the ones that the universe will reflect back on you. Two opposing vibrations cannot be within the same vibrational frequency according to the law of constants, which is part of the law of attraction; you cannot be happy and sad at the same time. To put this into perspective, energy particles are divided into different strata and zones. When you are exploring the details, you will find that depression and positivity is going to fall in different areas. Rather than choosing to stay stressed and be sad about being obese, you should rather be hopeful and optimistic and even believe that you are slim and think like a slim person.

Think and feel that you have the body that you love and your weight is exactly perfect. You should cherish the pleasure of having a perfect body and imagine that you are totally happy with who you are. When you feel happy, you will have your energy aligned to losing weight. With this kind of mindset and perception, you will start experiencing lesser challenges relating to your implementation of different weight loss techniques. You don't just have 100% belief that you will lose weight and continue eating unhealthy and not doing what you are supposed to do to lose weight. Actually, if you continue that kind of lifestyle, you are vibrating an opposing energy that will make it impossible to lose your desired weight.

Remember that the energy that you expend even when it is energy that leaves you to join other energies created by the Law of Attraction, you need to be aware that energy lost is also calories lost and that all of this helps you to get to being that person that you know yourself to be on the inside. Think how wonderful it will feel when what you see in the mirror matches that which you feel inside! It is perfect magic and you help it along the way by using the vision board as your inspiration.

Enter the Vibrational Zone of Achieving Weight Loss

As explained earlier, all matter has energy that vibrates at a particular frequency. Each vibrational frequency has a vibrational zone. Your current vibrational zone is the current zone you are moving in. When you focus your attention on the vibrational zone you want to enter (perfect weight) you life will reflect your move into the zone by displaying harmony with it. Each time you focus your energy on losing weight and having your dream body, you are changing your current vibrational zone. This simply means that you need to focus your attention on your achieving your goal weight since you will start moving into this vibrational zone.

This helps you considerably to stay focused. The energy being produced during the process of thinking is important. It must be positive energy for it to work. One doubt can screw up the whole procedure, so believe in yourself entirely. If you do find yourself thinking one negative thought, all you have to do is start again thinking in a positive manner and as you practice more and more, you will find that this will help you to be where you want to be.

When my daughter was younger, she had a terrible problem with puppy fat. We used this method on her because the natural energies really can help to distribute the weight a little better and also encouraged her to get beyond her negative thoughts about herself. These help no one, least of all the person who is trying to lose weight. We made a vision board together and I taught her to use it and from then on, I really didn't have to interject much at all because she could see where she was heading and enjoyed the trip.

She lost quite a bit of weight but she did this mostly by tuning in to positive energy and using this to keep her acting in the same way that slim people act. It worked and she is still slim and beautiful though to us, as parents, she was never anything else. Once we had her believing in herself, the struggle was over and the Law of Attraction latched onto her energy and helped her to find her way through all the self-doubt to a place where she really could look at her vision board and know that she was indeed the person she saw on the photograph she had placed there as her ideal.

Nathan Powers

Chapter 7 - How Vibrations Infusions Can Help You Lose Weight

Simply put, vibration infusions are due to your body interacting with vibrations that differ from your own thus infusing a vibration in your body that differs from that of your own. What this means is that every thought you have is a vibration infusion that will change your personal vibration and the more you may be exposed to a particular vibration, the more its vibrational frequency will be infused into your personal vibration and the more you will become like it.

To put this into perspective, the more you think about your losing weight and how good you will look, the more the vibrations of being fit will be infused into your personal life. Over time, you will start sending out vibes that represent what you will want to look like meaning that you will start to eat well and even exercise without too much effort because the vibrations of fitness and an appropriate weight are being infused into you.

This is a time when you really do need to feel close to your vision board as this helps you to really feel in the right frame of mind and as such your vibes will take perfect alignment with how you want to appear.

You also need reinforcement from your vision board because this also means that vibrations infuse and make you think differently about the way that you treat your body, how much food you consume and the way you want to look and do look on the inside. See yourself as beautiful if you are a woman or handsome if you are a man and never let anyone tell you differently. Once you start tuning into the changing vibrations within your body, you will follow their call and getting the shape you want to be will automatically follow.

Difficult Manifesting and How It Can Affect Weight Loss

Do you know that the greater the frequency you would difference between your current vibrational frequency and the vibrational experience were your desires met, the more difficult it would be for you to manifest your desires? Your goal should thus be to reduce the difference between your current vibrational frequency and the vibrational frequency you will attain were your desires met.

What this means is that any step you take towards improving how you feel so that you can feel that you have already lost weight will make it easier for you to start perceiving that your desire will bring fruits. For instance, in weight loss, small steps like reducing your intake of sugar make you feel good since you are making a step towards achieving your goal. Over time as you make various small changes in your life, you will start to see that it is not so hard after all to lose weight. This is where your power lies; the more you reduce you difficulty manifesting, the more you enter into your path of least resistance. What this means is that you will experience the least resistance as you continue in your journey of losing weight leading your achieving your goal weight.

How Baseline Thought Vibrations Affect Your Desire to Lose Weight

The thoughts that you always go back to even after having positive thoughts play a great role in determining whether you will be successful in losing weight. If you have positive thoughts of achieving your goal of losing weight for just a short time but go back to your sad mood since you are overweight, you are doing yourself no good. In order to change your baseline thought vibrations, meditation will be very important since as explained earlier on, meditation enables you to focus on selective things. Changing your baseline thought vibrations will enable you to lose weight especially if your baseline thought vibrations focus on how you have achieved your goal weight.

Collect Your Desires

Have you started buying those figure hugging clothes that you would want to wear once you achieve your goal weight? If not, you had better start buying those clothes. You may think that this does not make sense; however, you need to know that there is power in buying these simple items. You may even have started buying that bikini that you would want to wear once you shed off the pounds but did not even know that you were using the law of attraction.

You may probably wonder how buying something that you desire to wear once you lose weight will help you. Each time you collect an item that would be crucial in manifesting your desires; you are simply increasing your harmony with that of your desires. This makes you feel more and more as you would feel having lost that weight. As you continue to increase harmony with your vibrations, you increase the chances of losing weight.

Use of Counter Thoughts to Deal with Negative Thoughts

Getting rid of negative thoughts can be quite tricky since in most cases, we never want to have negative thoughts but somehow we find ourselves having these negative thoughts. If this is you, what do you do if you cannot seem to get a hold of your thoughts? You can consider using meditation. However, if you are still unsuccessful, the best option will be to use counter thoughts. Counter thoughts are very important since you generate a positive thought having the same subject matter as the negative thought. For instance, if you think of how you may get sick, you can instead think of how healthy you will be. If you think of how you would not start eating right because you seem to love fatty foods, you can start thinking instead of how you can start taking tasty meals from more healthy ingredients.

The more you practice how to deal with negative thoughts, the easier it becomes to have positive thoughts. This means that the more you think of how you will lose weight and look attractive, the more this actually becomes a reality.

If you continuously use counter thoughts and still find yourself unable to concentrate on what you want to achieve, the best thing would be to do something to get away from vibrations that may be entering your environment. For instance, when going to work, you can put a pair of headphones. The headphones will muffle any vibrations in your surrounding allowing you to concentrate on what you want manifested in your life; weight loss. Each time, you are having a hard time concentrating on your desire to lose weight, just put a pair headphones to help you start concentrating on how beautiful and healthy you would be once you lose all that weight.

Think of negative thoughts as roadblocks that stop you from getting to your final destination and by countering these straight away with good thoughts, you can still keep your goal in mind and achieve it. Negative thoughts don't work with the Law of Attraction because the energy that negative thoughts produces is not conducive to improvement. Thus it is wasted energy. You know that you can overcome temporary problems because you have come this far already, and the way to do that is to use your vision board and really believe in yourself as a person that you can trust.

You are a wonderful person and once you understand how all of this works, there will be no limit to the things that you can attract toward your life. The Law of Attraction doesn't just mean that you can attract weight loss. You can attract friendship, lovers, the kind of lifestyle that you always wanted and just about anything you set your heart on once you have learned to higher your energy levels by believing in whatever it is that you are trying to achieve.

Nathan Powers

Chapter 8 - Applying The Law Of Apparency In Weight Loss

When it comes to losing weight by successful application of law of attraction principles, you need to be familiar with the law of apparency. This is one of the most important parts of the law of attraction principles, as it will give you an insight into how you can make the most out of this principle.

Apparency simply refers to the degree to which you are apparent to something because of your current perspective. To make things more clear, this law states that the more you think of something, the more apparent it will become to you.

If you keep thinking that you weigh what you desire, it would be more apparent to you that you can be slender and you immediately start to feel the change manifest in you. As per this law, you need to give in to your desires and let your life be ruled by them completely. Do not let your desires remain locked up in a corner of your mind otherwise you will be vibrating the wrong kind of energy that will bring undesirable manifestations. You should give your desire the ability to control and spread over your thoughts. You need to believe in the possibility that the desires and cravings that you have are going to be a part of your reality; this in turn will inspire you to make things happen.

It becomes apparent to the universe that your thoughts need to collide with reality and soon you find yourself shedding all the extra pounds and attaining the perfect dream body. Things are really that simple, if you know how to keep your thoughts in control.

With this law and the other techniques to help you through, getting the dream body, which you have always coveted should not be a herculean task anymore. I will not ask you to expect the journey to be extremely smooth because our subconscious mind can be a very difficult thing to control. There are going to be too many conflicting emotions and thoughts and the more you try to control them, the far away they can wander. Therefore, you have to discipline your mind and go over these principals again if you want to see the results you want.

Believe it or not, this works but you need to be consistent. To manifest the weight that you want to be and the shape, you have to make sure that you concentrate on positive things at all times, even on days when you are not feeling up to your best.

Nathan Powers

How it works

The more your subconscious mind thinks of how good you feel about your light body, the more you vibrate desirable energies that bring back desirable manifestations from the universe. All you have to do is believe in the law of attraction, ask, believe that your desires will be manifested and wait for your manifestations. You then have to be receptive to the universe to receive your manifestations after which you should give thanks for such manifestations.

You are likely not to know when your desire to lose weight may be manifested. Additionally, you may not even know the thoughts that may have led to the manifestation of your current status. However, one thing you are sure of is how you would feel if you achieved your desired weight. As you continue manifesting in your desires, there is need to have faith in the process. Not having faith in the process will make all the efforts you may have put into having positive thoughts useless.

The first step to losing weight is to engage your mind. Do not expect to just make a decision to lose weight and succeed without involving your mind. As much as your mind is important, you also need to understand how you can use the laws of attraction to align your thoughts and mind to your goal of losing. Only then will you be able to achieve your goal.

Engaging your mind comes when you look at your vision board and know that you are thin on the inside and that you really do want your outside to catch up with you. There should be absolutely no doubt in your mind about it. Keep this to yourself if you want to because others do tend to sabotage our attempts at losing weight. It's not fair but it's part of how the world works. Keep that picture or those pictures in your mind all the time and think about what it's like to have lost that weight. Don't think in the future. Think in the now and imagine all that weight has gone. Imagine how you feel inside. Imagine how everyone around you will react and be very positive in your pursuit of that goal that you seek. The positivity that comes from you is what makes the Law of Attraction work.

If you look at this scenario, you can see why it wouldn't work for some people. Jenny is 42. She believes that as you get older you have no control over your weight. Her mother was like that and her mother before that. She doesn't believe she will ever be slim again and tried this method to see if it worked. She has also tried slimming biscuits, delivered meals and going to the gym once a week but none of that helped. She therefore has a very strong belief or mindset that tells her that nothing can work. Now, she is trying to use the Law of Attraction. She laughs at the idea of seeing herself as slim and when she looks in the mirror is very unhappy about who she is. She doesn't realize that your shape doesn't define you. She made the vision board, but because of her doubts as to whether it could work, the pictures that she placed on it were a little ridiculous and she knows she will never look like that. Within a week, she has declared the Law of Attraction as another failure. Why? Because she didn't do what the Law of Attraction says. No wonder her whole energy level was so low.

The point being made here is that you have to believe in what you are doing, use realistic pictures on your vision board and believe that you can reach those goals that you set for yourself. You are not going to be a Barbie doll overnight and the more realistic you can be, the more the positive vibes blend with the energies outside your body and help you to lose that excess weight. Miranda did the opposite. She used pictures a little slimmer than she was, totally believed in herself and within a fortnight had achieved the set weight and shape. She was so convinced about The Law of Attraction working that she went a step further. She then chose another image for her vision board that made her think a little harder and work a little more and worked toward achieving that kind of shape. By doing it gradually, she had more belief in herself and perhaps that's the way to do it if you find that you disbelieve the possibility of slimming down to your dream weight. Keep the images in proportion so that you can do it gradually if you think that you need to.

"I lose weight without much effort on my part at all," she told me. "In fact, I would say that just by being positive, I felt energies inside me that I hadn't felt for a long time and was able to expend more energy than ever before."

This is a great testimony from someone who tried the Law of Attraction for all the right reasons and succeeded. You too can make all your dreams apparent by not questioning what you are doing, and believing to the degree that Miranda did. It also works for men and there are several successes shown on YouTube that you may like to follow. These may give you more inspiration and help you to believe in what is happening to your body. The Law of Attraction is powerful but you need to believe in it without any doubts at all.

Chapter 9 – Keeping the Weight Off

One thing that yoyo dieters always ask me is whether this diet works like that. Will the weight pile back on again? The truth is that once you are slim, you will feel so great about it you won't want to backslide. Using the Law of Attraction to slim is different from using different diets because you chose the shape that you became. You had a clear vision of what you wanted to become and chose to become that shape. Thus, are you likely to backslide? It's unlikely because it was your belief in yourself that got you this far and the fact that you reached your goal reinforces that belief.

If you did start to backslide, it would be because of changes in your energy levels so you need to make sure that you keep to a lifestyle where those energy shifts are the same as they were while you were losing weight. In other words, the more positive you can remain, the more likely you are to stay at that weight. You will now be thinking like a slim person. You won't be tempted to pig out because slim people don't have the capacity to do that.

So how do you get to the stage where you feel bad about yourself in the first place?

You need to understand where all the bad feelings that you feel about yourself come from. During the course of your life, you judge yourself by your past experiences. It's all you have to go by. You may have been mocked at school. You may see little pockets of fat when you look at yourself in the mirror. The fact is that if you have had negative experiences, you tend to judge yourself by those negative experiences. You tell yourself "I am fat. I am ugly. I don't measure up" when you look in the mirror in the mornings and together with your bad experience, you allow this negativity to rule who you are. That's further reinforced by magazines that show you what you are supposed to look like until you dig a hole and jump in it because you don't feel you measure up to the standards of others.

When you think of it, it's perfectly natural that you will feel like this because it's how society has made you feel. You get a complex about yourself and tend to hide in clothing that doesn't show all those lumps and bumps because you think you look better. In fact, what you are doing is accentuating the fact that you are overweight. Then you comfort eat. This is something that people do when they feel bad about themselves. That small treat that feels so good on the lips is playing havoc with the hips but you don't care because you need something to make yourself feel good, with all the negative vibes that are surrounding you. It's very much a catch 22 situation when you get to this stage. You don't exercise. You watch a lot of TV and slouch on the sofa while treating yourself to snacks. The trouble is that millions of people get themselves into this rut every year and the figures at the moment of obese people are staggering.

They can't find a way out of the situation. They are too tired all the time because of the excess weight and thus have no energy for exercise. People continue to criticize them, so they continue to find solace in the only thing they know makes them feel great – and that's food.

You can see how people get to this stage, but when you decide you want to tackle it, you don't have to think in terms of starving yourself. That's the last thing that fat people want to do because that food is the only positive thing in their lives. If they deprive themselves of that, they feel there is nothing left to live for because every other experience of their lives is negative.

I've got news for you

All that a human being is consists of energy. You may feel lethargic, but that just means that the energy flow that you have isn't that good at the moment. It doesn't mean you can't improve it. The Law of Attraction allows you to use your natural energy to lose weight. It just happens but you need to change a few things before you can let it happen. For example, if you are one of those people who are constantly looking in the mirror and disapproving, stop it. Hide the mirror if you have to because all of this mirror watching is negative input and it's a bit like someone coming up to you every day of your life and saying "Hey there, you're fat!" That's not something that you need to hear. The problem is that all the feedback we get in our lives comes from people around us and make us feel the way that we do about our body, our behavior and our ability to measure up.

When you look into the mirror and disapprove, you are adding to all this negative feedback and making it worse than it actually is. Throw away the scales. They give you negative feedback. Get rid of them. You already know you are overweight and you don't need facts and figures to remind you of it. It's like the scales are joining in and saying, "Hey you're fat!" No wonder you turn to the cookie jar to find a little comfort. There is no comfort anywhere else. The problem is that the sugar high from the cookies only lasts a short time and raises your energy levels temporarily. You then take another cookie and the levels rise again, so you see eating cookies as a positive way to counteract all the negativity.

Can you see where all this is leading?

The cookie jar is your friend because it's the only thing that makes you feel good for a short time, but that short time is better than nothing. You see it as something that you deserve to feel. However, the sugar from the cookies soon wears off and all that is left is that fat you that everyone criticizes and that you constantly look at in the mirror and try to correct by wearing dull clothing.

Doesn't that tell you that something within this cycle of events is wrong? They are all logical steps. People make you feel bad. Cookies make you feel good even if it's only for a little while, but everyone needs that high occasionally, so you allow yourself it.

Now try looking at the whole situation in another way.

Get rid of the mirror. Stop trying to hide who you are. You are who you are. Look around you. Is everyone perfect? Of course not. There are those who appear perfect on the outside when they are actually not very nice on the inside. What you look like isn't the issue. The issue is that people are feeding you all this negativity about yourself and you are actually listening and taking it in. You reinforce what they say by picking on yourself every morning when you get dressed.

You need to see that your body is just the wrapping of the person inside. You have a mind and you have bodily functions like anyone else but what you are losing in this scenario is belief in yourself and positive energy and that's what is needed to make the Law of Attraction work. Remember the catchwords. Like attracts like. Thus, if you continue to allow yourself to be like this, the only thing you will attract is criticism because you criticize yourself. The only thing you are like to hear is negative because you believe that you merit it and you pick up on everything people say to you that is negative. You then do something even worse than that. You reinforce the negativity by looking at yourself in a mirror. It's not who you are. It's the body that you are in.

The vision board

The vision board is made so that you see who you think you are. This is the person that lives inside you. It's not the person that everyone criticizes and moans about. This is you. This is the real you. The vision board helps you to reach the real you if you are realistic about the pictures you choose to put on that board. Okay, you are not twig thin, but you are pretty beautiful and you like what you see.

You need to keep away from negative influences. If someone tells you that you are fat on a constant basis, that's not exactly the right material to have for a friend. They are negative and they are passing negativity to you. You don't need it any more. You are now going to only feed from positive energy. When you wake up in the morning you will look at your vision board and see yourself in the pictures you have chosen. You won't look in the mirror and you won't hide yourself away under layers of clothing.

You will begin to think in a very positive way. You may even find that the use of affirmations will help speed up the process. When you brush your teeth in the morning, look in the small mirror and tell yourself how beautiful and happy you are. You have to do this because the Law of Attraction only works on positivity. Now, take time to meditate on your vision board and face the world with a new confidence. People will notice the difference but they won't know what has made the difference. That's your secret.

Now, when you eat, think of that person on the vision board. What would she eat? What would make her happy? Think of exercise. What would she do? What would make her happy?

The whole point is that you have to drop all the negativity. This is the only way of raising your energy levels so that the energy levels of the universe are able to enter into and mingle with your energies and help take over the question of weight. It needs your help at first and you need to shed off all of the negativity that you have been fed for so long.

I remember one lady whose husband had left her because she wasn't the presentable woman that he wanted to show off to his bosses. The strange thing that happened following his departure was all down to the Law of Attraction. She got up one morning and decided that she was better off without him. There was no grief for the relationship. There was no bad reminder about how fat she had become. All she did was change her attitude. She didn't need someone as negative as him in her life and suddenly with his departure, all he negativity was gone.

Sitting down to lunch, she treated herself to foods that she would never have eaten had she been with him. She enjoyed salmon and a wonderful salad. In fact, she remembered that the only reason that she had ever changed the way she ate was because he insisted on fattening foods. Instead of feeling sorry for herself, she began to see who SHE really was inside and within weeks had shed a load of weight and was beginning to look really good. Why? Because she knew she wasn't a fat person inside and just wanted to go back to being herself. The positive energy she omitted allowed her to do that and in record time. The funny thing was that as she lost weight, her husband actually asked her back but she knew by then that he had turned her into something she no longer wanted to be and was happy with her life.

In future years, I remember her laughing about the fact that the woman he left her for, who was very slim at the time, was now every bit as fat as she had been and was walking around town with two kids. She saw the ironic side of it, but the reason she was able to get slim again was because she knew she wasn't this fat lump he had made her into. Using all of her positive thoughts, she put that right and anyone can do it, but they have to get into a positive mindset in order to do that.

That was one of the reasons I suggested that you see the person on your vision board as being you, rather than being what you want to be. See it as you. See it as the person inside trying to get out and the Law of Attraction actually mingles energies and allows this to happen. It really does. You have to let it in and you have send all the right messages and only positivity will do that as well as a very firm goal.

So, your first priority must be to throw off all the concepts from the past. Tell that packet of cookies that you don't need it to feel happy. You can manage to feel happy all on your own. Tell friends that criticize you that you don't need their negativity or simply walk away. Don't let them use you to feel good about themselves because that's all they are doing and it's awfully unkind. When people criticize others, they feel that it validates who they are. Forget it. You don't need to validate them. In fact, the fact that they were so critical validates that they are insensitive and unkind. Tell them that if you need to because you may just convert someone from being like this to realizing that what they said wasn't the kindest thing to say and showed them up as being insensitive and unkind.

Be proud of who you are and let the positive energy flow. You are no longer permitted to feel bad about anything. The thing is that all of these bad feelings are only thoughts and you control your thoughts. If you find yourself slipping back into bad thoughts, replace those thoughts instantly because you need to keep the positive energy flowing for this to work. I love me. Look at the picture on the vision board. This is whom I love. This is who I am inside. Convince yourself that the person on the board has the same figure as you have on the inside and allow yourself the positivity that you need to allow the Law of Attraction to work its wonders.

You may think this sounds a little hard to get your head around, but all of the thoughts you have about others come from inside you. If you don't' like who you are, you can't think happy and fruitful thoughts. You look at someone who is better than you and you measure yourself. Stop measuring yourself. Who you are isn't defined by who they are. Stop it in its tracks. If you can never learn to love yourself and see yourself as the person on the vision board, you will never be that person. You don't love yourself enough to have the energy that will take you there. So – you have flaws. We all do, but the person inside is the one that counts. Do you love her/him? You have to because if you are working toward being the person on your vision board, you have to trust the existing you to actually want to sit up and listen and be that person. If you don't love yourself, it's not likely to happen.

Nathan Powers

Chapter 10 – Where Thoughts Come From and What They Do

You probably think you already know the answer to this question, although chances are that you don't know how impermanent words and thoughts are. If you think a thought about yourself and it isn't very flattering, it can turn into many thoughts. Thought propagation is normal, but it's not necessary to human life. You add a chain of thoughts together. Everyone does it until they realize that they are totally in control of thoughts. Look at this destructive pattern and you may even recognize it:

- He doesn't love me any more
- I must be ugly
- I am not good enough

- She is better than me

- I am fat and ugly

- Why can't he love me for what I am?

Okay, it's a little bit overplayed, but you can see where I am coming from. But did you know that when you drop thoughts, that's the end of them if you want it to be. The reason we were so intent on teaching you meditation was so that you are capable of thinking of nothing. This was to help you to replace negative thoughts. Negative thoughts are your worst enemy because they keep you from reaching the Law of Attraction energies that will help you to lose weight. Thus, instead of thinking the thoughts that are written above, you need to be able to replace negatives with positives. I remember years ago watching a movie with Hayley Mills where she was a little girl who always saw a good side to everything. It's been my way of thinking ever since which is probably why I am such an optimist and believe in optimism. Even in dire circumstance, she was able to find a positive side of the situation.

You need to consciously replace negative thoughts with positive ones. We have already put away the mirror. We have already told you to get rid of people who you let into your life that put negativity there. Now all you need to do is replace all those negative thoughts.

- I left me so it's time to move on
- I will be able to do all the things I couldn't do with him
- I won't have to listen to his criticisms
- I can eat breakfast at 11 if I want to (use something he wouldn't let you do)

Yes, it's hard to put positive pictures on things that are bad, but it's possible. There are always positives and negatives to every situation. People tend to drown themselves in the negative because they feel they have lost something when a relationship breaks up. In fact, what they have gained is another chance at freedom, another chance at feeling all those nice things you feel at the beginning of another love affair, and the chances are that you have also gotten rid of all the things that your partner did that stopped you from actually doing things you wanted to do.

This is even true in the case of being widowed. One woman that I knew that lost her husband felt terrible of course, but she decided to sort her life out. After 45 years of being married she suddenly discovered that she actually didn't like a lot of the things that her husband liked. Over the years she had put up with them. Sorting through their record collection, she began to see the evolution of their relationship and how little parts of her were lost along the way. Yes, she had been very happy and was glad to have been married to the guy. She loved him, but inside her was this person who had been trying for years to get out and now it could.

We all go through negative thoughts but a thought is simply that – an abstract moment. Switch off your negative thoughts about yourself as soon as they happen and look at your vision board to remind you of who you are inside. You need to do this at regular intervals because negative people can't profit from the Law of Attraction.

The basic premise of the law of attraction is that like attracts like. If you are miserable, you invite misery. If you are happy, you invite happiness. If you are progressive, you invite progress. Thus, looking forward to that person coming out is all that you are concerned with and that's a really positive thing to happen. You have the potential. You are not asking your body to be anything other than what it is. You are just waiting for your outer body to match your inner body and once the Law of Attraction energies realize this, they will give you all the help you need to get there.

If you tell a child that he has the makings of a champion, he feels like a champion inside of himself and can work toward letting that champion surface. If you tell a child that he is useless, he will become useless because he believes that's all that you believe him to be capable of.

Get used to the fact that you are beautiful or handsome and that you have the potential to be this wonderfully slim person and you will become this slim person. You may not be exactly like the picture on your vision board, but your shape will be as near to perfect as it is capable of getting.

What to do to counter negativity

Negativity is the worst thing that can happen at this moment in time. In fact, negativity is always a bad thing. You need to stem it within your life and replace it with positivity. It sounds very simple and in fact it is once you get into the habit of doing this. You see, negativity is a little like stepping on your dreams. It's as bad as lying, cheating and being very ugly inside. Tell yourself, every time that you are negative that you are committing a sin against yourself and to stop it.

Energy is high on the agenda when you are asking help from the Law of Attraction. It is this high energy that mixes with the energy of the universe that helps you to get where you are going and to fulfill all of your dreams, hopes and ambitions. If you don't believe that, look at the way that Buddhist monks meditate. They are trying to reach perfection in their meditation process because they believe that when they reach perfection they will have arrived at Nirvana, which is their highest state. Think of it a little bit like reaching a high that you have never reached before. For them, it's meeting their inner soul or god and that's very important to them. I don't know enough about Buddhism to explain that any better, but I do know that in their meditation, they are heading for that place of possibility where energy flows together with the energy of the universe.

You need to aim toward simply feeling energy that is positive. That's not such a hard task, but if you find yourself going backward sometimes, you need to stop for a while and do a little meditation, using this method.

Sit with your back straight. It doesn't matter whether you cross your legs or take up one of the yoga positions. That's not what meditation is all about. It's more about finding the balance of the body so that the spine is straight. You head should be slightly raised because it makes sense that if your airways are open, you can breathe in a better way.

Your choice of place to meditate should always be somewhere away from distractions. Thus, if you need to close yourself into your room, then do so. I find that natural environments are perfect like being beside the sea or in an empty park, but the last thing that you need is the sound of children playing or anything that interrupts your line of thought and concentration until you are more familiar with meditation. We brushed on the subject slightly in an earlier chapter but now it's time to do it properly to ward off negative thoughts.

Make sure that your clothing is comfortable because you don't want distractions at all and a tight waistband is certainly a distraction. Close your eyes and breathe in through the nose concentrating totally on the breathing and nothing else. Let the air sit in your lungs for a moment and then breathe out being conscious of the air leaving your body coming from the upper abdomen. Count one on the exhale.

The only thing that you should be thinking about when you are doing this is the breathing itself, the upper abdomen and the count and each time you exhale the count goes up one all the way to ten. When you reach ten, you go back to one again. When you think of something you shouldn't be thinking about, you go back to one again.

You can safely do this for about quarter of an hour to start off with, but as you become more practiced at it, you will find that you can last up to three quarters of an hour and that you will feel refreshed when you do that.

Another way of breathing

If you are lacking in energy, this breathing exercise helps to build up your energy again and may be just the trick, especially when you are trying to keep your energy levels up. Sit in the normal pose for meditation and place your thumb on your left nostril. Breathe in through the right nostril and hold the breath. Then place your thumb on your right nostril and breathe out through the other nostril. This is a great way to energize yourself and you can repeat it up to 10 times.

After you do meditation, never just jump up and get back to your life. Take your time so that the body and the breathing get back to the normal rate slowly. You need to do this to benefit fully from the meditation process.

The reason I have introduced this into the picture is because it's a good way of getting rid of negative energy, which is of course not recognized by the Law of Attraction and will not help you in your quest to become slim. Thus, it gives you a distraction in a very positive manner and makes you get back to concentrating on what's important rather than being sidetracked and failing in your mission to become slim.

Meditation will help you through all stages of your life and helps to lift your spirits. It also helps you to fine tune the energies from your body and your mind so that you are not confused and can do all of the things you need to do to become that person you have pictured on your vision board.

It may interest you to know that businessmen who have multi-million dollar businesses have visions too. It is the vision that keeps them focused and that's the reason that the vision board was invented, to keep you always focused on your goal so that you know where you are going and how to get there without being distracted by life.

Often when people are trying to lose weight, they sabotage their own chances by letting their minds go off on tangents and think negative thoughts. All of these negative thoughts stop you in your tracks. Think of them in the same way as you think of swearing. You wouldn't do that too much would you? So treat negative thoughts in the same way so that you see them as something that's really not acceptable.

Nathan Powers

Chapter 11 – Food, Drink and Exercise

You can get results without incorporating too much change to diet, drink and exercise but believe me, you will do it more quickly if you incorporate all three. For example, water is a wonderful substance. You may think that you are drinking it by the bucketfull because you drink coffee or tea. You would actually be wrong. When you one cup of coffee, you urinate three cups! What that means is that all the excess water in your body that makes muscles pliable and strong will be depleted. Thus drinking water helps to put that balance right. Water is essential to life. If you have to drink it under sufferance as many people do, close your eyes for a second and pretend it is coffee. The power of thought is sufficient for anyone to do that and it's only for a few moments.

You may wonder where I am going with this chapter because the Law of Attraction can surely alter your energy fields sufficiently to make you slim, but when you think slim you do change the habits of a lifetime and this is part of the natural progress. You can't pig out too often when you are slim because your whole digestive system will shrink as well and won't hold as much as it did when you were fatter. Thus, slow adjustment to new amounts of food and drink are important, as well as knowing which foods can help you in your quest to become lithe and lovely.

I also said the word "exercise" which may have made you cringe, but exercise doesn't have to be negative either. Do you like dancing? Dance yourself silly with a Zumba tape and you burn calories. That slim person inside you loves dancing and using a jump rope and is a fun person who knows that exercise isn't' punishment. It's merely a way to expressing all that excess energy and it's good for you.

So what foods are really helpful in your quest?

Fish such as salmon is great because of all the Omega 3 that it holds. Okay you may not be able to afford it every day of the week, but it's delicious and will open up your taste buds to healthy food that doesn't have to taste dull. Lean protein helps you and that means things like white chicken (without the skin) or even shrimps. At 8 calories each, these are great for helping you to lose weight. Egg whites can also help you but if you eat an occasional omelet, the yellow won't hurt. If you try to cook using a spray rather than pouring oil from a bottle, this will also help. Get your body in tune with new tastes and experiment with foods you haven't tried yet. Whole grain bread is always a better bet than white and egg and cucumber sandwiches with a little light mayo are delicious. Use salsa and you will find this is less calories and can be used to spice up loads of different dishes.

You may be wondering why we are putting emphasis on food if the Law of Attraction is going to make you slim. The reason is that the food you eat also helps in the fight against getting bigger. Since my daughter started to experiment with different foods during her weight loss, she found that she actually liked some things that she had always avoided in the past and that keeping to these foods helped her considerably to gain energy and vitality and to keep her body in tip top condition.

The foods that you need to avoid the most, you already know. Potatoes in any large quantity are giving you too much starch. Similarly white bread isn't the best for you, although if you are capable of limiting the amount, can't do much harm in smaller quantities. Avoid cakes and all the obvious things, but allow yourself a little taste now and again to keep up your morale. This isn't about deprivation or diet. It's about your body getting to produce positive energy, which allows the energy of the universe to spur it on to losing the weight that you so badly want to lose.

In fact, don't even mention the word diet. A diet is a restriction and it's not about restriction either. It's about getting your body ready for the Law of Attraction to work its magic and starting to take a little bit of responsibility for the difference between your vision board image and the image that people see now. Nice foods really do motivate you and a bit of exercise makes you feel more physical energy, which leads you to the Law of Attraction working much more efficiently and quickly and if you want to see fast results, there's really no substitute.

This book is aimed at helping you to use the Law of Attraction, but do watch some of the videos on YouTube because people who have done this and succeeded really can give you the impetus you need to succeed in the same way as they have.

Conclusion

Thank you again for buying this book! It is part of a series that I have prepared on the Law of Attraction, which is a firm part of the life that I live. My intention is that these books will help people to find their own levels of success in each of the fields covered.

I hope this book was able to help you to know how use the law of attraction to lose weight. It will certainly give you food for thought. You don't need other people's approval. You don't even need to mention your weight loss efforts to others. When you succeed, however, feel free to share that success with friends because there may be something very positive you can do for them to help them overcome their problems. The Law of attraction works in many areas – not just weight loss – and once you take the reins and see the power that it unleashes, you can have a very happy and eventful life that uses everything that you learned for your benefit.

Once you do, you will see a vast difference in your approach to life and will also notice that people around you become more positive toward you. The positivity of the Law of Attraction is the one thing that you will always take with you on your journey through life and it will help you to realize your hopes, dreams and aspirations by focusing you on the areas of your life that you wish to improve. Use your vision board. See that vision and remember that you are that person you see. All you need to do now is become that person. The book shows you how.

The next step is to start doing something about what you have learned in the book and start to feel the benefits that the Law of Attraction puts into your life. It's amazing. It's there for everyone to grasp at and use, though those that don't take advantage of this natural phenomena lose out on the opportunity of a lifetime.

Check Out My Other Books

Below you'll find some of my other books that are popular on Amazon and Kindle as well. Simply click on the links below to check them out.

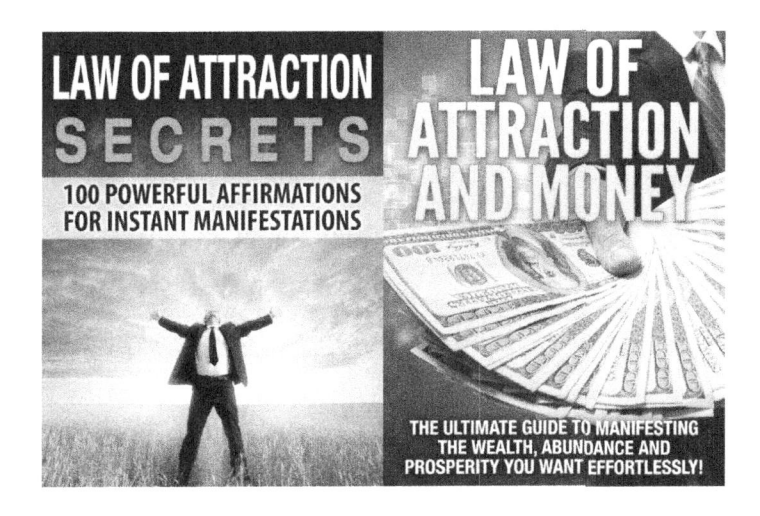

Law of Attraction Secrets – 100 Powerful Affirmations for Instant Manifestations

The Law of Attraction and Money – The Ultimate Guide to Manifesting The Wealth, Abundance and Prosperity You Want Effortlessly!

Preview of: "Law of Attraction Secrets – 100 Powerful Affirmations for Instant Manifestations"

The law of attraction and affirmations

We are all products of our thoughts whether we like it or not. Our current state is a product of our past and present thoughts. As part of the universe and as part of matter, which is all infinite energy, we attract the energies that we vibrate. This means that if we vibrate the right kind of energy, we can attract whatever we want instantly. The more you believe or want something to happen in a certain way that is different from your current state, the more you start manifesting that which you want. In this case, you will have infused vibrations that match what you want resulting to you attracting what you want. Each of your thoughts is a vibration infusion that determines how your personal vibration will be; the more you expose yourself to a particular vibration, the greater its vibrational frequency will blend into your personal vibration resulting you and your life becoming more like it. As the saying goes, like attract like!

Although you can use different strategies to infuse vibrations that are different from your current state and expect manifestation, affirmations stand out as strong tools that help you vibrate the right kind of energy that matches what you want resulting to you attracting that which you want in your life. Knowing which affirmations to say and how to transform your mindset to start vibrating the kind of energy you want to manifest is essential if you are to receive your manifestations instantly. Remember, your affirmations should be focused on the end (what you want to manifest) and not the means (how you want to get the manifestations of what you want). Simply put, forget the means and focus on the ends throughout your affirmations. The more you focus on the means, the more your perceived difficulty in manifesting will be. On the flipside, having the thinking that your desires are being fulfilled changes your vibration to match what you want manifested in your life. It also changes who you really are and whatever it is you experience and perceive to match the manifestation of your desires.

The law of attraction focuses on three simple steps; ask (in this case affirm), believe, receive (be observant to notice the manifestations) and be thankful. Even as you say the affirmations outlined in this book, following these simple steps will keep the manifestations coming. Affirmations and the law of attraction go hand in hand. The more you affirm that something is going to happen in a certain manner, the more it will become a reality in your life. For instance, the more you affirm how much you are in love with someone, the more you will feel the love you have for them and the more you will feel that your lives revolve around each other. This will make you have more experiences that relate to the feelings you have for them. Likewise, if your affirmations relate to them being happy, the more the experiences that relate to being happy you will have. In simple terms, the more your attention is focused towards certain life experiences that you want in your life, the more of those life experiences will manifest in your life. The more thought you give to your desires, the more apparent those desires will manifest in your day-to-day life. If you affirm whatever you want in your life, you start moving into a new vibrational zone; this is referred to as vibrational immersion in the law of attraction. Do you know that if you purposely focus your attention towards entering into a new vibrational zone, your life will start changing in a manner that reflects your close interaction with your intended vibrational zone? Affirmations allow you to focus your attention towards the vibrational zones that you want manifested in your life allowing you to continuously transform your thoughts and perceptions that match with the vibrational zone you want manifested in your life. If your desired experiences manifest in your life, you can actually use vibrational locking to keep attracting that which has already manifested in your life. Vibrational locking entails knowing your vibrational frequency at the time of manifestation of certain wants to allow you to experience more manifestations in your life.

Affirmations are actually some of the best tools you can use to counter negative thoughts about things you don't want in your life; in this case, your affirmations should be positive. Don't just affirm that you don't want something to happen; say what you want to happen instead. This is the best way to start vibrating the right kind of energy that will attract the manifestations you want in your life. We will go through 100 affirmations that will change your life by allowing you to manifest anything you want instantly. For easier learning, I have divided the affirmations into situations in which you can say them to get the manifestations you want so badly in your life.

Nathan Powers

Made in the USA
Monee, IL
23 February 2023